Father Aloysius:
Wonder Worker in America

Father Aloysius:
Wonder Worker in America

by Jeffrey J. Moynihan

Queenship
PUBLISHING COMPANY
P.O Box 42028 Santa Barbara, CA 93140-2028
(800) 647-9882 • (805) 957-4893 • Fax: (805) 957-1631

Dedication

This book is dedicated to Jesus Christ present in the Most Blessed Sacrament, to the Blessed Virgin Mary our Heavenly Mother, to Father Aloysius and to all the priests throughout the world today who work for the salvation of souls. - JJM

Acknowledgments

The author wishes to express his thanks to the following. Each contributed photographs, information, or assistance in some form towards this book. They include Father Charles Carpenter M.A.P., Mother Marguerite Carter (Carmelites of Fallbrook), Sister Johanna Murphy S.S.C.M., Mrs. Judith Albright, Mrs. Anne Marie Carroll, Mrs. Mari Naty Castro (who is a niece of Father Aloysius), Mrs. Mary Lou De La Hoz, Mr. Francis Levy, and Mr. & Mrs. Robert Queen.

Library of Congress Number # 96-69105

Published by:
    Queenship Publishing
    P.O. Box 42028
    Santa Barbara, CA 93140-2028
    (800) 647-9882 • (805) 957-4893 • Fax: (805) 957-1631

Printed in the United States of America

ISBN: 1-882972-75-9

Contents

Endorsements of Father Aloysius

(quoted from letters)

"Thank you for informing me of your intention to write about Father Aloysius Ellacuria, C.M.F. He was a friend. Best wishes."

Most Rev. Justin Rigali,
Archbishop of St. Louis,
May 16, 1995.

"I knew Father Aloysius only by sight. Many, many people used to go to him for spiritual counselling. I knew that he had some special gifts."

Very Rev. Donald Montrose,
Bishop of Stockton, California,
November 30, 1995.

"I will always have a grateful memory of Father Aloysius Ellacuria, C.M.F. He radiated the presence of Our Lord, especially when recollected in prayer before the Blessed Sacrament. The way he pronounced the prayers from the depth of his soul convinced one that here was a true man of God."

Monsignor Joseph Herres,
Pastor of San Antonio de Padua,
Los Angeles, California,
December 22, 1995.

CHAPTER 1

The Many Wonders

God tells us through St. Paul in Sacred Scripture (the Holy Bible) that some are given "the grace of healing ... the working of miracles ... prophecy ... discerning of spirits." (1 Cor. 12:9-10) In the opinion of many people, these gifts were given to Father Aloysius Ellacuria C.M.F., (1905-1981). In their opinion, he should be a possible candidate for sainthood. Of course, it is only Church authority, after intensive investigation, that judges if someone should be canonized a saint or not. Therefore, Church authority welcomes personal testimonies of people who knew the possible candidate for sainthood.

It is with joy that I say that I knew Father Aloysius very well. I was his full-time volunteer helper, his first personal secretary, his driver, and his Mass server for a whole year (from August 1968 to July 1969). I lived in his same rectory house, worked in his same office, and ate at the same table with him. These events all took place at Immaculate Heart of Mary Parish, 617 South Santa Rosa Blvd., in San Antonio, Texas.

That wonderful year I had with Father Aloysius gave me the opportunity to get to know him as few others did. He became my spiritual father, and he told me many things about his life and his mystical gifts.

The gift that impressed me the most was his gift of reading of the soul, also called "reading hearts." This gift falls under the "discerning of spirits." It instantly reveals all hidden thoughts and secrets of a soul. Reading hearts is mentioned in the Bible: "The secrets of his heart are made manifest; and so, falling down on his face, he will adore God, affirming that God is among you indeed." (1 Cor.14:25) The Church says this gift is truly supernatural. It is a miracle of the mind.

Father Aloysius told me he was given this gift to help people. He used it to help counsel them. He also used it to help people make good confessions. Christ commanded the hearing of confessions when He told his apostles; "whose sins you shall forgive, they are forgiven them." (John 20:23) In confession, if someone either forgot or hid a sin, Father Aloysius would use the gift to tell the person what he was omitting. Father would say the circumstances involved to help the person remember. The person would then make a complete confession and leave happily, with peace of mind. In the past, other confessors who have had this gift include: St. Thomas Aquinas, St. Philip Neri, St. Joseph of Cupertino, St John Vianney, and Padre Pio.

I asked Father Aloysius when and how he was given this gift. He said he was given it on Holy Thursday (March 21) of 1940. At that time, he had been a priest for 10 years and was 34 years old. He had this gift for the next 41 years of his priestly life, until his death in 1981. The details of how he received it will be explained later in this book in Chapter 4, "The Golden Rays."

Father Aloysius proved to me many times that he had this gift. It always really amazed me when he did. Although I had previously received a quick blessing from him twice before in Los Angeles, I never had an opportunity for a conversation with him and to see his powers. Finally, the first time for me to have a private talk with him came in August 1968. As we sat talking in his office, he read my whole soul all in an instant. He could see that I knew he had this gift (or power). So, he began proving it to me. He told me: "You're thinking of becoming a married deacon." No one knew that except God and me. Father's choice of words he used was perfect. Thinking about was correct because I was not planning to. Nor did Father say I "would be" a married deacon. He was right; because I am married today, but I am not a deacon. There were many other times Father Aloysius read my soul.

Father also saw that I had come to San Antonio to be in a volunteer group that helped poor parishes. Although I was already assigned to begin work at another parish, Father asked me to request a transfer to his parish to be his helper. To my surprise, the group granted my request. I was then able to live and work at Father's parish and help him.

In those first days there, Father and I went out for walks around the parish grounds in the evening. Once while walking, he told me:

"The other day when I read your soul, I was surprised to see you have a mistaken idea about Christ. You think Christ has only a human body united to His Divinity. Christ has a human soul too, and you don't know that." I was amazed. I had never spoken to anyone about that. I realized that Father could read the soul to its very depths, down to the smallest details of what the soul knows (or does not know) about God. Again he had proven his ability to read souls to me.

A few days later, Father gave me a cassock (black robe) to be worn for serving Mass. I thought to myself: "The last time I wore a cassock was when I was in the seminary. I liked to wear it." Father smiled at me and said: "You're thinking that the last time you wore a cassock was in the seminary and that you liked wearing it." This is an example of Father seeing thoughts at the same moment they are produced. But he could also easily see thoughts produced at an earlier time. For example, one day Father suggested I take a break from the office and do a little gardening for relaxation. While doing it, I thought to myself: "I might like to become a Claretian priest, like Father." Later, at lunch, Father turned to me and said: "This morning in the garden, you were thinking you might like to become a priest. The Claretians would be happy to have you!"

Later that year, I was thinking that I was unworthy to be a priest. Therefore, I thought that maybe it would be nice to be a religious brother and start an order of them with great love for Christ in the Blessed Sacrament. I would name them: "Brothers of the Blessed Sacrament." I didn't say a word to anyone about this idea. Later that week, Father smiled at me and said: "I like your idea about you starting a group of religious. I also like the title you would give them: Brothers of the Blessed Sacrament." I was amazed because Father saw the exact words I formed in my mind, but never had spoken with my mouth.

Most amazing to me was that Father could even see the forgotten knowledge filed away in the soul. Father proved this to me when he told me about something that happened when I was only three years old. He used it as an example of how our guardian angel protects us. He told me the incident, but I could not remember it. After Father died, the memory of it returned to me. It was exactly as Father had described, as if he had seen a video or movie of it.

3

Of course, there are many other witnesses who received proof from Father that he could read souls. Among these witnesses are Father Alberto Ruiz C.M.F., Father Kevin Manion C.M.F., Father Charles Carpenter M.A.P., Mrs. Josephine Pue, Mr. Michael Murphy, and Mrs. Milagros Jimenez. There were probably at least several hundred people who received proof of this gift, during the 41 years that Father made use of it in his priesthood.

Father could see everything that was already in the soul by means of the gift of reading souls. But he could not see the future of the soul, because that is done by another gift. Father called that other gift: "the *full* gift of prophecy." He said that very few are given it. He told me that two people who had that gift were Sister Mediatrix and Mother Esperanza, who will be described later in this book.

Father did at times get a glimpse of the future. He had what he called a *"limited* gift of prophecy." He proved this to me and to others. For example, in early January of 1970, Father prophesied that I would have a nephew born "before next Christmas." Eleven months later, in November of 1970, my first nephew (named Mitchel) was born. Father also prophesied that several different people would be cured "by next Christmas," and they were.

Father was best known for his gift of curing. When he died, the Catholic newspaper for Los Angeles (called the Tidings) on April 10 of 1981 printed that Father Aloysius was "known for his healing ministry." There were probably at least several hundred people cured by God through the priestly blessing and prayers of Father Aloysius (over a period of 41 years). A few of those cured are Mrs. Dottie Harvey of cancer, Mr. Kyle Dennisson of Hodgkin's Disease, and Miss Lupita Jimenez of leukemia.

Father told me that the most amount of cures were of cancer. But there were also cures of leukemia, diabetes, blindness, asthma, arthritis, etc. There was even a case of distorted facial features slowly changing into a normal face over a period of several weeks. As for myself, one day I had a very bad headache. Father blest me, and my headache instantly disappeared.

Not everyone who came to Father was cured. Father prayed hard that everyone would be. But he said it was God Who made the choice of whom to cure. Father said it was a mystery. But he also said that in cases where the person died soon after coming to him, it was because God wanted that person in Heaven with Him.

Besides physical cures, Father helped bring about many spiritual cures. By means of his reading souls, giving blessings, and prayers, Father helped many people. Many people felt a wonderful feeling go through their soul the moment Father blest them. I know I sure did when he blest me!

Through Father's intercession many lapsed Catholics returned to the practice of their Faith, with a greater love for God. Father Aloysius also converted a number of people to the Catholic Faith. Among these were: Miss Dorothy Hulen, her mother, and her brother Kenneth, who was cured of asthma.

Father also had the gift of mystical aroma. It is a sudden, powerful and beautiful scent like roses. Pope Benedict XIV judged mystical aroma to be truly miraculous. It has happened with holy people down through the centuries. This most pleasing smell shows how pleased God is with the person He gives it to. Many people experienced it in the presence of Father Aloysius. These include: Father Alberto Ruiz C.M.F., Mother Marguerite, myself (once), and many others.

Father also had the gift of luminosity. This is the giving off of a special light. It includes when an aura is seen. An aura was seen behind Father's head at times as he said Mass. Several people told me they had seen it and I am sorry that I did not record their names. I was also told that a blue light was seen shining around Father's hand as he held the rosary.

As for myself, one night I saw a bright gold star appear next to Father's room, and a blue star next to his office. I was 22 at the time, and had never seen anything special before in my life. It happened all of a sudden, and came as a complete surprise to me. I think that this is also a form of luminosity related to Father Aloysius' mystical gifts.

Father was said to levitate off the floor, up into the air on rare occasions. He seemed to do this at the elevation of the Host at Mass, but again, only rarely. In Italy, two holy priests who also levitated at the elevation of the Host were: St. Gaspar (1786-1837) and St. John Bosco (1815-1888).

The only time that it definitely seemed to me that Father was off the floor was in October of 1968. It was at the elevation of the Host at the Shrine of the Most Merciful Love, at Collevalenza, near Perugia in Italy. Father had just met and read the soul of Mother Esperanza (1893-1983). She was originally from Spain, but founded her order in Italy. She was very famous for her gift of prophecy, and the pope went to see her several times. Pope John Paul II made a public visit to her on November 22, 1981, in front of thousands of people.

Father Aloysius was so moved by what he saw in her soul, he began to cry during his Mass (just after meeting her). I was serving Mass for Father, and noticed at the elevation, his body slowly rising upward compared to the top of the altar. He must have levitated 4 or 5 inches off the floor. I did not look down at his feet, although he was right next to me. I felt it was not respectful to take my eyes off the Host to look elsewhere out of curiosity. The altar was between us and the 50 people in our pilgrimage group. Thus, the altar blocked the view of father's feet to others. However, several people (such as Mrs. Morrow) noticed Father's body slowly moving upward over a period of 10 to 15 seconds at this mass. He then slowly came down as he lowered the Host to the altar.

On another occasion, one witness definitely did see Father's feet off the floor, about 4 inches up in the air. That person was Mother Marguerite at the Miraculous Medal Shrine in Paris. It was on the 1975 Pilgrimage. She told me she was up in front at a side chapel, as Father said Mass. She said there was no one in front of her (except Father) and nothing blocking her view. She told me she clearly saw him really levitate up in the air, and I have no doubt that he really did this.

Since Father had these various mystical gifts, one cannot help but wonder how he came to have them. In order to know how this happened, one must go through Father's life history in the proper sequence of time.

The author, Jeff Moynihan, with Father Aloysius at
Immaculate Heart Parish in San Antonio, Texas, in June of 1969.

CHAPTER 2

His Early Years

F ather Aloysius was born in his parents' farmhouse on June 21, 1905. This was at the small town of Yurre in Vizcaya Province, Spain. Yurre is located about 15 miles southeast of the city of Bilbao on the road to Vitoria. I was there in 1976, and noticed that it was in the green, coastal area of northern Spain. I saw pine forests on the mountain sides. Father told me that the pine tree was his favorite tree, because it reminded him of his home.

Yurre is in the Basque country. The Basque people have their own language, which is very different from the Spanish language. Father spoke Basque at home as his native language. Later, he learned to speak Spanish at school. He, his brothers and sisters, all attended the Carmelite School at Yurre. Unfortunately, years later, that school was closed during the Spanish Civil War (1936-1939).

The father of Father Aloysius was Mr. Ramon Ellacuria (1873-1920). He was born and baptized on Christmas Day, December 25, 1873, at Yurre. At age 24, he married the mother of Father Aloysius, her name was Miss Marta Echevarria (1874-1950). She was born and baptized on July 29, 1874 at the town of Ceanuri (located about 10 miles southeast of Yurre). She too was 24 years old on the day of their marriage, September 10, 1898. They were married at her parish church in Ceanuri.

Ramon was a farmer who owned his own house, fields, orchards, and pastures. He was a very spiritual person. He died of pneumonia on February 20, 1920, at the age of 46. Father Aloysius was fourteen and at the Claretian Minor Seminary at Valmaseda. The seminary was strict at that time and did not permit Father Aloysius to return home for his father's funeral and burial.

In Spain, it was also the custom in those days to save land in farming communities by keeping the cemeteries small. Thus, after several of years of burial, the bones of a person would be dug up for reburial in a small corner of the cemetery. When Ramon was dug up for his reburial, his family was surprised to discover his body to be perfectly incorrupt. This is a rare grace that God gives only to a very few.

Marta (the mother of Aloysius) died of hemiplegia, which is paralysis from a stroke. She died on January 1, 1950, at the age of 75 (the same age Father Aloysius would be when he died). When it came time to rebury her remains, Marta was found to be corrupt as only bones (as is natural). Father Aloysius felt his mother was in Heaven, and as a proof of it, he called upon her intercession to cure a lady with advanced cancer. At that same moment of his call, the lady's cancer was cured with a feeling of fire going through it. To Father Aloysius, this cure was a sign that his mother was in Heaven.

In Spain today, the custom of reburying human remains is being discontinued. To save land and space, the new custom is to stack coffins four high in walls along the sides of a cemetery.

Father Aloysius was born into a large family. He was one of nine children. He had four brothers and four sisters. Their order of birth was: Maria, Hipolita, Julia, Father Aloysius who was called Juan Luis, Marcelina, Ignacio who died as a young man, Father Jose Maria, Nemesio who died at ten months old, and finally Francisco. None of them is still living today. However, sixteen of their children (who are nephews and nieces of Father Aloysius) are still living.

Father's home town of Yurre has the parish church of St. Mary of the Assumption. In that church, Father was baptized as John Aloysius or Juan Luis in Spanish. Father had been born on the feast day of St. Aloysius Gonzaga. In the parish church Father was baptized when he was one day old, received his First Holy Communion when he was almost seven years old, and had his Confirmation when he was eight years old.

I asked Father if he ever noticed anything supernatural as a child. He said, "yes." At times he heard the miraculous sound of wings hovering above his head at night, when he was in bed. For him, this sound was a sign of the presence of his guardian angel.

Father told me that as a child he always knew he wanted to be a priest. He first thought of becoming a cloistered Carmelite, because of his devotion to Our Lady. But one day, he heard a Claretian missionary priest speak at his parish church. He spoke about St. Anthony Claret and the Claretians. Father then decided to join the Claretians, instead of the Carmelites.

At the age of eleven, Father and three other boys from Yurre entered the Claretian minor seminary at Valmaseda (located west of Bilbao). Father was a student there from the age of eleven to fifteen. While there, a priest told Father: "If you give yourself completely to God, He will work miracles through you someday."

At age fifteen, Father and his classmates went by train to the novitiate at Salvatierra in Alava Province. At the beginning of this novitiate year, Father received his religious habit (the typical cassock or black robe). At the end of this novitiate year, at age sixteen, he was very happy to make his first profession of temporary vows as a Claretian.

Father and his classmates then took the train to the Philosophy Seminary at Beire, in Navarra Province. There, they spent the next three years in the Philosophy Program at that school.

Next, they went to the Theology Seminary at Santo Domingo de la Calzada, in La Rioja Province. There, they studied Theology for three years. While there, some Castillian seminary students made fun of Father and his Basque accent. Christ was mocked during His life on earth; so too was Father Aloysius at this seminary.

While there at the seminary, in 1925, nearby at the town of Ezcaray, a beautiful, golden, Spanish baroque altarpiece was prepared for shipment. It was later shipped to the Los Angeles area of California. This was, in a sense, a prophecy of where Father himself would soon be sent to spend most of his priestly life.

That same altarpiece later ended up in the chapel of the diocesan minor seminary for Los Angeles, Our Lady Queen of Angels Seminary. I was to see it myself for three years while being a student there. In fact, I was to see it the same day I met Father Aloysius for the first time in September of 1961. The same altarpiece that had been so close to him in Spain, during his seminary days, was once again close to him in Los Angeles, and at the seminary I was then attending.

Today that altarpiece continues to be in the same chapel. However, the seminary is now closed and is being used by Alemany Catholic High School. Alemany moved there because of earhquake damage done to its original campus buildings. The former seminary (now Alemany Catholic High School) is located next to the old Mission San Fernando at Mission Hills, California. Because of its great beauty, the altarpiece might be moved into the new cathedral, being planned for Los Angeles. It is planned to be built during the next few years.

Also when Father was at the Theology Seminary at Santo Domingo de la Calzada, he made his perpetual profession of vows as a Claretian. This he did on June 22, 1926, the day after he turned 21 years old. The next year, in 1927, from this seminary, Father received his Licentiate Degree in Theology.

Father's next step was the Moral Theology Seminary at Segovia. There, he spent the next two years studying moral theology and Canon Law.

After this, came Father's final step to the priesthood. It was at Aranda de Duero, in Burgos Province. There at the Claretian Inter-Provincial Seminary, he completed the one-year program called Ministerial Preparation. His studies included Pastoral Theology. During that year, Father was ordained a priest on November 3, 1929 at Burgos, by the Archbishop.

The ordaining of priests is done by the "laying on of hands" (on the head). It is seen done in 1 Timothy 4:14, Titus 1:5, and Acts 14:22.

Being ordained a priest, Father Aloysius also received the title "Father." Some Protestant churches object to this title, pointing to Christ's words: "Call none your father on earth" because God is your Father. (Matt. 23:9) Here Christ spoke figuratively, not literally. He emphasized that no father on earth is as much a Father as God in Heaven. Christ is also figurative when in Matt. 5:29-30 He said: "it's better to cut off your hand" or to "pluck out your eye" instead of using them for sin. That was a figurative emphasis against sin. It is an exaggeration to make a point. It was never meant to be really done. Christ goes on to call fathers on earth "Fathers" in Matt. 15:4-6 and elsewhere. St. Paul calls spiritual fathers "Fathers" in 1 Cor. 4:15-16. This quote is the reason the Catholic Church calls priests "Fathers," because they serve as spiritual fathers. Thus, Father Aloysius received his name: "Father Aloysius" in English or "Padre Luis" in Spanish.

Priests offer the Eucharist because Christ commanded the apostles (and their successors): "Do this in memory of Me." (Luke 22:19).

Thus, to carry out this holy command of Christ, Father Aloysius began his priestly life in 1929.

Father Aloysius as a child. He received his First Holy communion when he was almost seven years old.

Father Aloysius with his mother Marta, when he was 24. He is seen here in 1929, just after being ordained a priest. They are seated in front of their home at Yurre.

The Ezcaray Altarpiece - a prophecy
Father's future destination.

CHAPTER 3

To America

After he was ordained a priest, Father Aloysius completed his final ministerial preparation. He was then notified that he was being assigned to Panama. However, a Claretian seminary in Compton, California, known as Dominguez Seminary, requested they be sent a young priest who could teach Greek, Latin, and Spanish. Since Father was excellent at these languages, plus a young 24 years old, the office of the Claretian Father General in Rome assigned Father to Dominguez Seminary instead. He was also told that this assignment to the Claretian Province of the United States would be for the rest of his life.

At that time in 1930, U.S. Immigration Law accepted foreign clergymen only after they had already been ordained for two years. But the law also counted the time as an ordained deacon as part of those two years. Since Father had been ordained a deacon on February 23, 1929, it meant his two years would be up in February of 1931. Thus, Father was meanwhile assigned to Panama for six months to await his entry into the United States.

Father went by ship from Barcelona and arrived in Colon, Panama, in early October of 1930. He immediately went to Panama City, where he was assigned to help out at the Cathedral. On Sundays, he acted as pastor at Taboga Island, located about 15 miles away.

During his six months at Panama City Cathedral, Father became friends with the bishop, Bishop Preciado (who was also a Claretian). This bishop was later helped by Father Aloysius, when Father arranged for him to visit the Chicago area. There, the bishop was able to receive donations and even volunteers to help him with the Indians in Panama.

In April of 1931, Father went by ship from Panama to the United States. He arrived at San Diego, California, on April 25, 1931. He arrived here in the United States at the young age of 25. He quickly learned to speak fluent English and became an American citizen. He was to spend almost all of his next 50 years as a priest in his new country.

Father said it was a big sacrifice for him to give up his homeland, his family, and even his native language. But he knew that such a sacrifice would be pleasing to God. Thus, Father said that he was happy to do it.

When Father arrived at Dominguez Seminary in April of 1931, it was still a fairly new place. It had been built only four years earlier, in 1927. It was named after the generous Dominguez Family, who had donated all of the land and much of the money to build it. There, Father taught Greek, Latin, and Spanish. These were the main subjects he taught during his teaching years. He taught at Dominguez Seminary from 1931 to 1933. From 1933 to 1935, he taught at another seminary called Claretian College, which was located at Walnut (also in the Los Angeles area). Claretian College previously had been a guest ranch, called Silver Peak Ranch. Today it is a golf course and no longer a seminary.

From 1935 to 1942, Father was assigned to teach at St. Jude's Seminary at Momence, Illinois. The town of Momence is located 50 miles south of downtown Chicago. Today St. Jude's is no longer a seminary. The building is now called Good Shepherd Manor, and is a home for 120 mentally retarded men. I am glad that the building is being used for this good work. My own job is working with the mentally retarded and severely handicapped. I feel this kind of work is charitable by nature, and pleasing to God. I hope that this good work may be continued in that building for many years to come.

During Father's last years at St. Jude, something wonderful happened. It was at this time that he was given his mystical gifts. It will take a whole chapter to explain how this happened.

CHAPTER 4

The Golden Rays

A lthough Father Aloysius had been at St. Jude's Seminary since 1935, he had other duties. During his last years there, from 1939 to 1942, Father became the confessor for a few convents in the local area. In doing so, he met a mystic who changed his life completely.

In 1939, Father became the confessor for the four nuns living and working at Our Lady Academy at the town of Manteno, Illinois. It was located about ten miles northwest of St. Jude's Seminary at Momence. Also living with these four nuns was a staff member named Miss Frances Hennessey (1911-1959). She had been in the novitiate of these nuns, but was forced to leave because of poor health. So, during the year of 1938, she went to live and work at Our Lady's Academy in Manteno. Miss Hennessey also went to confession to Father with the nuns at the academy.

Father Aloysius told me that Miss Hennessey was a mystic, who really had the gift of prophecy. Father first met her in 1939, when he became her confessor. She told him that he would soon receive the gifts of reading souls and of curing the sick. The very next year, in 1940, her prophecy came true, and Father was amazed. In 1939, Our Lady's Academy was a school with 75 students. A number of them lived there as boarders, but most of them were from St. Joseph's Parish next-door. During Holy Week, all of the students were at home. Thus, on Holy Thursday of 1939, Father Aloysius came to say Mass in the academy chapel for the nuns and the staff only. On that day in the chapel, Father received a mystical experience, called "conforming union." In it, God prepares a soul for later receiving the transforming union. When Father received this grace, Miss Hennessey was present and perceived that he received it.

The next year, on Holy Thursday (March 21) of 1940, Father again said Mass in the same chapel. It was customary then to say Mass in the morning on Holy Thursday, and not in the evening as is done today. That Holy Thursday, Father was to receive his greatest gifts from God.

Father told me that after saying Mass that day, he came out of the sacristy and knelt down in front of the tabernacle, some distance from it. He was giving thanks, when suddenly he received the "transforming union." He saw golden rays of light. These rays came out of the Blessed Sacrament, through the tabernacle door, and straight to the heart of Father Aloysius. At that moment, he received the gift of reading hearts and of curing the sick. He was filled with indescribable joy, and he felt like he was inside of God.

Father Aloysius was not the only one present who saw the golden rays from the tabernacle. He said several others there saw them too. He said that Miss Hennessey was one of them who did. He didn't tell me who the others were. But, for various reasons, I would guess they were Sister Margaret Mary and Sister Mary Catherine. Father Aloysius told only a few people about the golden rays, including Father Charles Carpenter M.A.P., Mr. Michael Murphy, and myself. Father was so very humble that he very rarely spoke about himself, (even less about his gifts), and only when asked by myself or others to do so.

After seeing the golden rays, Father could see the souls of people, with their secrets and all. However, he did not realize he had also received the gift of curing. Although, Father did not perceive it, Miss Hennessey had. In some ways, she was a greater mystic than Father was. So, she told him about his other gift of curing. To prove this to him, she sent two ladies, with severe arthritis, to request his blessing. He reluctantly blest the ladies, and they were instantly cured. This was the first cure that God worked through him. Now with the knowledge of his second gift, Father continued the healing ministry of Jesus in his own priestly life.

Father's gift of curing seemed to have helped Miss Hennessey too. For with Father's blessings, her health was restored to her. She was then able to re-enter the novitiate, and complete it successfully. This was with the same order of sisters who were at Our Lady's Academy. The sisters are called the Servants of the Holy Heart of Mary. Their Latin initials are S.S.C.M. They were founded in 1860 in Paris, France. They first came to the United States to Kankakee County (south of Chicago) in 1889. They later had their Provincial House and Novitiate built with their Holy Family Academy. There was one chapel to serve the academy, the provincial house, and the novitiate. The academy was located at the small town of Beaverville, Illinois, about fifteen miles south of St. Jude's Seminary at Momence.

With her health restored, Miss Hennessey re-entered the novitiate at Beaverville on May 31, 1940. She was given the name Sister Mary Mediatrix. While she was there, Father Aloysius was also confessor for their community. While Father was saying Mass in the chapel on Holy Thursday (April 10) of 1941, he received another mystical gift called "Sacramental Species." This is when the Communion Host (the Blessed Sacrament) remains miraculously intact in the stomach and is not digested until the next Holy Communion. Thus, a person's body becomes a "living tabernacle." Father was probably in ecstasy at the moment he was given this grace. He did not perceive it, but Sister Mediatrix did. She told him about it. To prove it to him, she told him to call on Christ present within him to cure someone. Father did just that a number of times. Each time, the person was miraculously cured, proving this grace. Sister Mary Mediatrix had again made known to Father a grace he had received from God.

Sister Mediatrix also made the prophecy to Father that he would have a long life, but one of suffering. Both of these things later came true.

Because Sister Mediatrix was so special in Father's life, something should be said of her life. She was born in Chicago on June 4, 1911, as Miss Frances Hennessey. Father pointed out to me that she was of Irish descent. Father told me: "Miss Hennessey was Irish, just like you."
Frances had one sister and several brothers. They grew up together on the northside of Chicago. One of the parishes they lived in was that of St. Ignatius. She later became a discalced cloistered Carmelite with the name of Sister Teresa, after the Little Flower. After being a Carmelite for some time, she was forced to leave because of poor health, and before she could make any final vows.

Frances heard about the Sisters of the Holy Heart of Mary from her close friend, Johanna Murphy, who had already joined them. This order would be easier on her health because they did not have the severe diet and sleeping hours that the cloistered Carmelites had.

With her health improved, Frances entered their novitiate at Beaverville on June 29, 1936, with the name Sister Mary Grace. There she then became friends with Sister Gertrude Marie Kare. Before she died, Sister Gertrude, with painful arthritis in her hands, wrote out a long eight page letter about Frances. She pointed out in the letter that Frances was forced to leave their novitiate because of poor health. Frances then helped at St. Mary's Hospital in Kankakee.

After her health improved, Frances entered the novitiate again on November 20, 1937. This time she was fine until Lent of 1938. Then she became very ill, as if in a mystical way. Sister Gertrude visited Frances and said she looked like the suffering Christ.

The novitiate told Frances to leave again because of her poor health. She was greatly disappointed, but accepted it with resignation to God's will. It was then, at this time in 1938, that she went to live and work at Our Lady's Academy in Manteno.

Sister Gertrude goes on to write that it was there at Manteno that "many beautiful things happened to Frances ... one in particular, that she received the invisible stigmata. One of the Sisters was present, Sister St. Phillip." The moment of receiving the invisible stigmata was also possibly the moment she received her gift of prophecy. This had all happened in 1938, so as to prepare her for her encounters with Father Aloysius in the following year. Thus in 1939, she would be able to make a prophecy to Father about his soon-to-be mystical gifts of 1940.

Of course, one of the "beautiful things" that happened to Frances at Manteno was her seeing the golden rays of light come to Father Aloysius from the tabernacle. She also saw a silver cloud of light turn gold as it entered Father. Another beautiful thing was that her health was restored through Father's blessings, which finally enabled her to become a nun.

When Frances re-entered the novitiate on May 31, 1940, it was for the last time. This time she was given the new name: "Sister Mary Mediatrix." After successfully completing the novitiate at Beaverville, she made her first vows on August 15, 1941. She was then assigned to continue at the novitiate as a Sub-Mistress of Novices.

In 1942, Father Aloysius was reassigned to California. So, Sister Mediatrix lost Father as her confessor. But, by that time she had already changed Father's life completely. He had become a mystic, just like her.

The next year, in 1943, Sister Mediatrix was assigned to a girls' boarding school, called Villa Maria. It was located next-door to St. Patrick's Academy at Momence, the same town where Father Aloysius had been assigned to for his previous seven years at St. Jude's Seminary. At Villa Maria, Sister was in charge of the girls' dormitory. She was also a teacher's aide at times.

On August 15, 1947, Sister made her final vows as a nun. Later, during the 1950's, she had to endure some persecution. There were some who misunderstood her. One Mother Provincial destroyed some of her files and ordered the other sisters to destroy whatever they had written down about her. For awhile, Sister Mediatrix was not permitted to speak to any of the other sisters, except for one. Through this though, she remained cheerful and charitable.

Sister did have some health problems at times. Finally, she came down with cancer. At that time, in the late 1950's, she was in charge of the kitchen at St. Patrick's Academy at Momence.

At the age of 48, Sister Mediatrix died of cancer (carcinoma of the large intestine). She died on June 9, 1959, at St. Mary's Hospital in Kankakee. On June 12, she was buried at Beaverville at St. Mary's parish Cemetery located just behind St. Mary's Church (and to the left). St. Mary's Church,because of its large size and artistic beauty, is called the "cathedral of the cornfields." It is certainly worth a visit.

St. Mary's Cemetery is open to the public. The tomb of Sister Mediatrix would be an excellent place to ask her for her intercession in Heaven. If any miracle is obtained, a testimony of it should be sent to:

Provincial Superior
Servants of the Holy Heart of Mary
145 South Fourth Ave.
Kankakee, Illinois 60901

The Servants of the Holy Heart of Mary have not yet done anything to open investigations for a Cause for Sister Mediatrix.

However, they should do so, because they have no canonized saint in their order. With Sister Mediatrix, they could have a wonderful possibility.

After Sister died in 1959, her order changed somewhat. In 1968, they stopped wearing their religious habit. Later, in 1972, Father Aloysius wrote to Sister Margaret Mary about this. He wrote: "They tell me that your Congregation is not the same anymore. How sad it is. I do love your Congregation regardless, and pray for you all."

Father felt that all religious orders should wear a religious habit. He called it "God's uniform." In the case of the Holy Heart of Mary Sisters, they at least wear a small religious emblem on their clothing. It has a blue background with a cross on it. These sisters continue to do many good works today. They staff St. Mary's Hospital at Kankakee, and also do social and educational work. In the late 1950's, they moved their Provincial Residence from Beaverville to Kankakee, near St. Mary's Hospital. At Beaverville, their old Provincial House, Novitiate, and Holy Family Academy, have all been torn down. What now remains at Beaverville is the order's cemetery. It occupies two different sections of St. Mary's Cemetery. There remains the tomb of Sister Mediatrix, a place that I hope will someday become a place of pilgrimage. Like Father Aloysius always said: "The Almighty God can do all things," and if He desires the canonization of Sister Mediatrix, it will be.

Our Lady Academy at Manteno was also torn down, by orders of the Fire Department. Only one small building of it remains, the former laundry building. It has been converted into classroom use for catechism. Near this building is where the chapel of the golden rays used to be. It was a large chapel on the second floor of the academy. Today, the exact spot is an open, outdoor, park-like setting, on the grounds of St. Joseph Parish. St. Joseph Church is next to the area. This place too, hopefully, will become a place of pilgrimage. There should be a recognition of the miracle of the Golden Rays. It was a beautiful miracle, done by God. It was done right here in the United States, in the very heartland of our country.

Father Aloysius proved to me many times that he could easily read souls. When he told me this gift came to him from the Blessed Sacrament, it proved to me even more that Christ is truly present in the Blessed Sacrament. It also further proved to me that my Catholic Faith is the one true Faith.

This gift was given to Father in the heartland of a country, where most people are not Catholic. Protestants outnumber Catholics here. They often verbally attack Catholic truths by misunderstanding the Bible. For example, they deny that the Blessed Virgin Mary, Father Aloysius, Sister Mediatrix, and others in Heaven can intercede on our behalf. They point to the Bible where it says Christ is the "one mediator of God and men." (1 Tim. 2:5) What they don't realize is that intercession prayer is to and "through Christ." (Romans 15:30) The intercession of the Blessed Virgin Mary is with her Son. On earth, she asked Him for a miracle for others (the changing of water to wine) and He granted it. (John 2:1-11) Just as she could ask Him on earth, she likewise can do so in Heaven. Asking the Blessed Virgin Mary for her prayers in Heaven is the same as when St. Paul asked others to help him by their prayers. (Romans 15:30) The Bible clearly states that "prayers, intercessions ... are good in the sight of God." (1 Tim. 2:1-3) It also states that "in Heaven ... the prayers of the saints went up before God." (Apocalypse/Revelations 8:1-4)

Another error that I have had to hear a number of times is about the status of the Blessed Virgin Mary. Most Protestants downgrade her status. The Bible clearly states that Christ is God: "The Word was God ... and was made flesh ... and lived amongst us." (John 1:1-14) Thus God was made flesh inside the Blessed Virgin Mary. She is the Mother of God. Christ is only one person with two natures (God and man). The Blessed Virgin Mary is the mother of the one person of Christ, thus the Mother of God. The original Greek does not say she is simply "highly favored." It literally says she is "fully graced." (Luke 1:28) This status of the Blessed Virgin Mary is only one of many things that so many in our country do not understand.

In their attacks on Catholic truth, many Protestants also condemn religious statues and images. They point to where the Bible says that images are not to be made for "adoring and serving." (Exodus 20:3-50) Leviticus 26:1 makes it clear that nothing is to be made in order "to adore." Adoration is for God alone. Of course! Statues and images are not "adored" by Catholics, but are used for religious inspiration only. God commanded the making of images (statues) for the purpose of religious inspiration. This is seen when He commanded (for the Ark of the Covenant) that there be made images in statue form of cherubim angels with wings and faces. (Exodus 25:18-20)

It would take too long here to go into all the mistaken ideas that fill this land of ours today. The good thing is that in all this darkness of error, there is still preserved the light of truth. The golden rays of light came forth from God in the heartland of our nation. That golden light was the light of His truth.

Sister Mary Mediatrix S.S.C.M., the former Miss Frances Hennessey, made very correct prophecies about Father Aloysius' life.

*The chapel at Our Lady's Academy in Manteno, Illinois, as it looked in
1940. On Holy Thursday (March 21) of that year, Father Aloysius,
and the others saw golden rays of light come from the tabernacle straight
to his heart. At that moment, he received the gift of reading hearts and
of curing. The tabernacle is seen in the very center of the photograph.
Above and behind it is a statue of Our Lady of Victory with the Christ
Child. In this same chapel, Father Aloysius used to hear confessions.
The gift of reading hearts is something very useful in hearing confessions.*

*View of the convent section of Our Lady's Academy at Manteno, Illinois.
The school section is seen behind the convent.*

*The chapel of the Provincial House, Novitiate, and Holy Family
Academy at Beaverville, Illinois. In this chapel, on Holy Thursday
(April 10) of 1941, Father Aloysius received the gift of "Sacramental
Species," making him a "living tabernacle" of Our Lord Jesus Christ.
A statue of Our Lord is seen above the altar.*

*The Provincial House & Novitiate, the chapel (upper floor of the center
building), and Holy Family Academy at Beaverville, Illinois. All three
buildings were connected together.*

CHAPTER 5

His Guardian Angel

In 1942, Father was transferred back to California to be Master of Novices. Claretian College at Walnut was now the novitiate, and had need of him. Later, from 1943 to 1948, Father was again assigned to Dominguez Seminary. Today it is no longer a seminary, but serves as a retirement home for Claretians.

From 1948 to 1957, Father was again assigned to be Master of Novices. However, the novitiate property at Walnut had been sold, and the novitiate had moved to the large property at the Provincial House in Los Angeles. This property is located at 1119 Westchester Place and includes a whole city block. It was originally donated to the Claretians by Dr. Del Amo, who married Susanna Dominguez of the famous Dominguez Family.

While he was at this new location as Master of Novices, Father had another wonderful thing happen. His guardian angel materialized as a policeman to help him. I first heard of this incident in October of 1968. Miss Evelyn Gavin (1901-1994), who was a papal countess from Cleveland, Ohio, told me about it. She heard of it directly from a witness, named Mrs. Tillie Hair, who was a friend of Father's for many years. Evelyn and Tillie felt that I should know about it, just in case I should ever see Father's "policeman" myself. As it turned out, I did see him.

In Tillie's case, she had driven Father to Santa Teresita Hospital to hear the confession of a dying lady. Father had to be back to lead the novices in the Angelus Prayer at 12 noon. Since Father had taken so long at the hospital, it looked like it would be impossible for them to get back on time. As they walked out of the hospital, they saw a policeman sitting on his motorcycle. He took off his helmet out of respect for Father and asked if he could be of service. Father told him that he had to quickly return to the novitiate. The policeman then drove ahead of the car to each intersection on the way back to the novitiate and waved Tillie's car through. They made it back just on time. Tillie told Father that it was certainly strange how that policeman had just happened by, and that she thought that policeman was the most handsome man she had ever seen. Father answered: "That's not a man! That's my guardian angel!" At that moment, the "policeman" smiled at them and disappeared right before their eyes.

St. Thomas Aquinas wrote that angels materialize by condensing the atoms in the air, and changing them into the form they want. Examples of this are in the Bible in several places, like when the Angel Raphael materialized as a young man to help young Tobias on his long journey.

It is believed that guardian angels have materialized to help other saintly people. The guardian angel of St. John Bosco is believed to have materialized as a large dog, a dog that never changed, nor grew old over a period of 30 years. This dog saved the life of St. John Bosco several times, and often came from out of nowhere to protect him.

I heard from Mother Marguerite of a second incident of Father's guardian angel becoming a policeman. This time Father was in the car with some novices, who had to be back at the novitiate within five minutes. Suddenly, a policeman on a motorcycle was in front of them. Father told the novice driving the car to follow the policeman. He did, and they made it back on time. It became known to a few that the "policeman" was Father's guardian angel.

After Evelyn told me about the first incident, I asked Father if it was really true. He nodded his head yes, and turned red with embarrassment. I had always wondered why he had been so embarrassed. Then, after Father died, the reason came to me. There had been a third incident with the heavenly policeman, and I had been there. But Father did not identify the policeman to me at the time, and thus he was embarrassed when I mentioned it to him later on.

This incident happened in September of 1968, when I drove Father for the first time. He told me that he once tried to learn to drive. But he always slammed on the brakes too quickly, making it dangerous for everyone. So he gave up and decided it would be safer if he had others drive for him.

On this occasion, I was driving Father in San Antonio. It must have been a Saturday morning because there was no traffic on the freeway. There was no one anywhere near us. Suddenly, there was a policeman on a motorcycle just to the side of my window. I thought: Where in the world did he come from? I had no thought that it might be Father's guardian angel, because it was not until a month later that I was to first hear about him from Evelyn.

The policeman speeded up so that he was next to my left front fender. He then looked back through the front window of the car at Father Aloysius. Father then turned his head to the left and saw the policeman staring at him. The expression on Father's face changed, as if he recognized him. He and the policeman just kept staring at each other for a few moments, as if they were talking to each other mentally.

Then the policeman speeded up again and rode his motorcycle directly in front of us, as if he were our police escort. I turned to Father and said: "That policeman looked at you like he knows you." Father gave me an evasive answer, saying: "The police have a lot of respect for priests." I then looked back at the policeman and he was now nowhere in sight, as if he had suddenly just disappeared. I told Father: "Look! The policeman is gone! Where did he go?" Father just answered: "Oh! They go so fast!"

I think that Father Aloysius knew his guardian angel very well. He once mentioned to me that, because of his special mission in life, he had been assigned three guardian angels. He said his main guardian angel was a Cherub, and that the two other assisting angels were a Principality and a Power.

Father Aloysius: Wonder Worker in America

CHAPTER 6

His X-Ray

B y the year 1957, Father Aloysius had become very popular in the Los Angeles area. So many people were coming to see him that it was beginning to interfere with his duties as Master of Novices. Thus, his superiors decided to let him give all of his time to the public. Father started twelve groups of volunteers, called Claretian Guilds. These groups included many people. They held monthly meetings and helped the Claretians with prayers and donations. The donations were used to help the Claretians with their foreign missions, home missions, seminaries, and with various other projects and good works.

Father was permitted to give individual blessings to the public in the Provincial Chapel, every Sunday afternoon, just after his public novena. There were many cures for those who suffered and sought Father's blessing.

As Sister Mediatrix had prophesied, Father himself was to suffer too. At times, he too became ill. He was in the hospital for a whole month in 1959. After becoming well, he had to return to the hospital again in August of 1961. This time it was much more serious than before. He was dying of a brain tumor. The doctors said he needed an operation to remove the tumor, or he would die. Yet, the operation, they said, would leave him without a mind, and just like a "vegetable."

Father's superiors felt that he had no choice and that he should have the operation to save his life. Thus, Father entered St. John's Hospital in Santa Monica on August 5, 1961. For several days, he prayed intensely to the Blessed Virgin Mary to intercede with her Son to cure him. Father's desire was to continue living in order to help save other souls. Father felt completely unworthy to receive any cure. But the one who feels unworthy is the one whom God chooses.

Father's prayers were answered on the night of August 10, the Thursday before August 15 (the Feastday of Mary's Assumption into Heaven).

The next morning, August 11, Father was scheduled to have his operation. When they came to prepare him for it, he told them to take another x-ray. He said his brain tumor was gone. Father also pointed out that the paralysis of the left side of his body was now gone. Father's doctor, Dr. McKenna, immediately had an x-ray taken. When Dr. Mckenna returned with the developed x-ray, he knelt down and told Father: "This is a miracle!"

The x-ray no longer showed any trace of the brain tumor he had earlier. It had been located on the left side of his brain. It was clearly seen on all the previous x-rays. Just the day before, it had been clearly seen. Now, just a day later, with no operation, the tumor was gone.

Father said the cure took place while he was praying the rosary. At the Second Joyful Mystery (the Visitation), Father felt the hands of the Blessed Virgin Mary on the top of his head. At that moment, he was cured. Her placing her hands on his head was the exact same method that Father used to help others. Father would place his hands on the heads of people who came to see him in order to bless them and to cure them.

Dr. McKenna had Father stay in the hospital for a little while longer in order to make a complete observation and to have him rest up some more. On August 26, 1961, Father checked out of the hospital, completely well and completely cured. By this cure, God saved and extended Father's life for another twenty years, from 1961 to 1981. Father was yet to live and work in a number of different places, even as far away as Fatima in Portugal. However, when Father finally died, providentially it was back at this very same hospital of St. John's in Santa Monica, California, that it happened. Father Karl Claver, who brought Father Aloysius Holy Communion two days before he died, confirmed to me that it was at St. John's Hospital that Father finally died.

By God extending Father's life in 1961, He made it possible for Father to meet and bless thousands of more people. Among them was me. Only one month after Father's cure, in September of

1961, I was able to meet Father for the first time. I was only 15 years old at that time. My parents brought me with them to Father's Sunday afternoon novena in the large chapel behind the old Provincial House. The chapel was completely full of people, with a long line of people also waiting outside. It finally came my turn to be blest. As Father blest me, I felt a wonderful feeling of graces in my soul. And that very special feeling stayed with me for several hours afterwards.

The Old Provincial House, where Father Aloysius lived from 1948 to 1963.
Behind it was the large chapel where Father blest long lines of people.

Father Aloysius: Wonder Worker in America

CHAPTER 7

The Queen of Egypt

The second time, I was to be blest by Father Aloysius, came to me as a surprise. It was in early 1963, when I was a student at the high school seminary, next to San Fernando Mission. Every six weeks, all the juniors and seniors would go home on a Friday for a weekend visit. There were four of us in my class from Pomona. Normally, the four of us (Doug, Sam, Philip, and I) would have gone directly home. But another classmate (named Ramon) asked us to drop him off at his home near downtown Los Angeles. Since he lived so close to the beautiful St. Vincent's Church, he offered to show it to us. Besides the church, he also showed us the mansions behind it, which are a part of the downtown campus of Mount St. Mary's College. As we walked in front of the Doheny Mansion, we were surprised to see my mother and Mrs. Morrow walking out of it with some other ladies. They had just finished attending a meeting of one of the twelve Claretian Guilds that Father Aloysius directed. They said that Father Aloysius was still inside, giving blessings to people as they left. Mrs. Morrow added that everyone there was excited because attending the meeting was Her Majesty, Queen Nazli (the former Queen of Egypt).

My fellow seminarians and I went inside the Doheny Mansion and into the ornate Pompeian Room, with its stained-glass dome and marble walls. There, we were all able to receive individual blessings from Father. Again I felt that wonderful feeling of spiritual graces come over me.

Mrs. Morrow then pointed out to us Queen Nazli and her daughter Princess Fathia. They were sitting together in front of us. They, too, noticed us, because we were dressed in our seminary uniforms.

Something here should be said about Queen Nazli, because she was the highest of the high society that came to see Father. She was born into the high society of Egypt as Nazli Sabri (1900-1978). She was the daughter of the Minister of Agriculture. In the year 1919, at the young age of 19, Nazli married Sultan Fuad. She thus became the Sultaness of Egypt. Three years later, in 1922, England gave Egypt its independence. The titles of Sultan and Sultaness were then raised to King and Queen. Thus, Nazli became the first Queen of Egypt since Cleopatra.

Nazli's husband, King Fuad, was more than just a figurehead. He had power, but not as much as an absolute monarch. The monarchy was very popular in Egypt, because it represented national pride and independence.

Their majesties had five children: a son Prince Farouk (1920-1965) and four daughters, with Princess Fathia (1930-1976) being the youngest. During the 1920's and 1930's, Queen Nazli and her family lived in the Abdin Palace in downtown Cairo. This palace had been built by Nazli's father-in-law (Sultan Ismail). It was one of the biggest and most beautiful palaces in the world, with over 500 rooms, marble walls, crystal chandeliers, and many other luxuries. Today it is an important government building, called the Republic Palace.

Because air-conditioning had not yet been invented, the Royal Family spent every summer at their palace on the cooler Mediterranean Sea coast, at Alexandria. As they left Cairo, they would ride in a special car in a royal parade, and were cheered by crowds of people as they went to the train station. On special state occasions, Queen Nazli would wear a tiara crown of diamonds, that was worth a million dollars.

Queen Nazli's husband, King Fuad, was king from 1922 to 1936. Then, her son, Prince Farouk, became King from 1936 to 1952. Her son King Farouk (1920-1965) was at first very popular with the people. But as the years went by, his life style changed into one of night clubs and worldly living. Queen Mother Nazli was unhappy with this, and came to live here in the United States. Later, in 1952, there was a military coup against her wayward son. He was forced out of office and out of Egypt. He went to live in Italy, where he died in 1965. The monarchy had existed for thirty years (1922-1952). Under it, there had been greater personal and business freedom than there was under the socialist military dictators that replaced it. These new rulers seized power by force, and not by a vote of the people.

In the United States, Queen Nazli first lived in San Francisco. Then, in the early 1950's, she and her daughter Fathia moved to the Los Angeles area (into a mansion in Beverly Hills). Later, they became friends of Father Aloysius and converts to the Catholic Faith. Previously, they had been Moslems.

Father Aloysius thought very highly of Her Majesty. She used to write to him in San Antonio, Texas. Father then had me type out letters to her from him. He told me: "She was Queen of Egypt for many years, and she is still every bit a queen. You never dreamed you would be typing letters to a queen!"

Queen Nazli was not the only Catholic celebrity to visit Father Aloysius in Los Angeles. During the 1950's and 1960's, other Catholic celebrities who went to see Father included: Conrad Hilton of the Hilton Hotels, Emmet Culligan of the Culligan Water Company, and the movie stars: Irene Dunne, Maureen O'Hara, and Loretta Young. Among bishops, Bishop Arzube and Bishop Moreno (Auxiliary Bishops of Los Angeles) were to become close friends of Father. They concelebrated Mass with him in 1979, at his 50th anniversary of being a priest. Today Bishop Arzube lives in retirement. Bishop Moreno is at present Bishop of Tucson, Arizona. Archbishop Rigali, who at present is Archbishop of St. Louis, Missouri, was also a friend of Father Aloysius.

Because Father had so many people coming to him, he attracted the attention of those who did not like him. The Devil, for sure, was not pleased that Father was drawing so many people closer to God. The Devil (it seems) wanted to put an end to all this. So there began a lie (a lie straight from Hell) that Father Aloysius was trying to start a cult to himself as a saint. In 1963, a small group of influential men took this lie to Cardinal McIntyre of Los Angeles. The cardinal decided to accept their recommendation of expelling Father from Los Angeles. Father then received a phone call from the Chancery Office, telling him he was suspended, with no faculties to function as a priest in this archdiocese. Thus, he was being sent into exile.

It was strange that I saw Father with the Queen of Egypt, just before this happened. Egypt was the land of exile for the Christ Child. And now, Father Aloysius, like the Christ Child, was going into exile.

Her Majesty, Queen Nazli, in 1950, when she was still the Queen Mother of Egypt.

CHAPTER 8

Into Exile

Father's Claretian superiors were totally unprepared for the news of his being suspended and expelled. In the past they had greatly benefited from his popularity. He had encouraged a number of young men, who later became Claretians. He had also obtained for the Claretians many donations of money needed for their work. One lady, cured of cancer by Father, donated half a million dollars to build the Claretville Seminary at 26800 Mulholland in the mountains near Calabasas. Today it is a school for learning Japanese, called Soka University. The Claretians now use a seminary in San Antonio, Texas.

It would be impossible to give all the details of how Father benefited his order, the Claretians. They in turn were grateful to him and wanted to assign him to a place of honor, outside of Los Angeles. There was no position for a superior open at that moment. So they sent Father back to Spain (to Bilbao) on an extended leave.

After a few months, there was an opening for a pastor at Immaculate Heart Parish in Phoenix, Arizona. This position was then assigned to Father. Phoenix was then in the diocese of Tucson, with Bishop Green as its bishop. He gladly welcomed Father into his diocese and even became his personal friend. Bishop Green also recommended to his diocesan priests, in Phoenix, to have Father Aloysius as their confessor.

In Phoenix, Father refurbished the church, rectory, and grounds of his parish. For this, he received a beautification award from the city mayor. This parish is located in downtown Phoenix. Years later, because of less vocations, the Claretians were no longer able to supply the personnel to staff it. So today, this parish is staffed by diocesan priests of the new diocese of Phoenix.

During Father's three years in Phoenix (1963 to 1966), he was able to have his younger brother (Father Jose Maria) be with him for a year. They both liked that very much. Also at Phoenix, Father performed many marriage ceremonies for couples who had been living together. Many people learned of Father's gifts and went to confession to him. Others received cures through his blessings. Thus, Father accomplished much good, while in Phoenix.

In 1966, Father was assigned for the next three years as superior and pastor of the Immaculate Heart Parish in San Antonio, Texas. Here too, he refurbished the church, rectory, and grounds of his parish. Likewise, he received a beautification award from this city.

While in San Antonio, Father received a lot of mail (mostly from California). A volunteer lady had helped him part-time to answer this mail. But suddenly, she left Texas to join a convent in another state. Father prayed to the Blessed Virgin Mary to send him someone to help him answer his piles of mail. It was at that moment (in August of 1968) that I stopped by to see Father. He asked me to become his full-time helper and I gladly accepted. He said the Blessed Virgin Mary sent me to him.

Since I had already taken typing classes, I knew how to type for Father. He told me it was the first time in his life that he was able to have a personal secretary. The parish secretary was too busy with parish business, and did not have the time needed to answer the piles of Father's personal mail. This became my first project there and within a month I had helped Father to answer it all.

My next project was to send out typed requests for donations for refurbishing the parish. This I did to all the 2,000 addresses of Father's friends and acquaintances. The response was excellent, and paid for most of the refurbishing.

In October 1968, thanks to financial help from my father, Dr. Robert Moynihan, I was able to be in Father's pilgrimage to Rome. In Rome , Father met Pope Paul VI.

CHAPTER 9

With the Pope

Our pilgrimage group was with other groups in St. Peter's Basilica to see the pope. Each group was permitted to have three people meet the pope and speak to him for a moment. From our group it was Father Aloysius, with Commander and Mrs. Hubka.

Father told me that when he met the pope, he had a mystical experience. He mystically felt as if he were in the presence of Christ Himself. Father said that he realized that the pope is not Christ. Yet, Father felt the presence and authority of Christ in the pope.

The Church teaches us that the pope is Christ's personal representative here on earth, and thus the leader of His Church. The pope is the Bishop of Rome. He is the only one who has ever claimed leadership over the whole Church, and the only one ever accepted as having such authority.

The claim is seen in the Bible when Christ promised to give special authority to St. Peter: "You are Peter ..." (Matt. 16:18-19) This authority is to be "on earth" as the quote says. Later, the authority is given when Christ commands Peter: "Feed my sheep." (John 21:17) Thus, Christ made Peter shepherd of the flock (the Church). Ezechiel 34:2 says the flock "is fed" by the shepherd. Thus, Christ (the Good Shepherd) gave the job of feeding the sheep (being the shepherd) to Peter.

After Christ's ascension into Heaven, the Bible shows Peter is accepted as leader of the Church. The Book of Acts shows Peter acting as leader in various ways.

Peter lived in Rome, where he acted as bishop. He was then martyred and buried there. There is historical proof of it. Each Bishop of Rome after Peter inherited his same office, and thus the position of leadership. Christ intended the Church to last "until the end of the world." (Matt. 28:18-20) Thus, the leadership of the Church did not die with Peter, but continued on through his successors. This was pointed out at the Church Council of Ephesus in the year 431. There it was officially recorded that it had been "known to all ages, that Peter, Prince and Head of the Apostles ... lives on in his successors, exercising judgment." Thus, Father Aloysius had a brief mystical encounter with one of those successors.

Father was very pleased with this pilgrimage of 1968. But after it, back in San Antonio, he again felt the sorrow of exile. He was now in his sixth year of exile, and did not know if it would ever end. Then, in the spring of 1969, the good news came. Cardinal McIntyre was granting an amnesty to the various priests he had exiled, because he was preparing for his retirement in January of 1970. Of course, Father's Claretian superiors, and thousands of people, wanted Father back in Los Angeles. So, he was re-assigned to the Provincial House in July of 1969. He was overjoyed. For me, being with Father in his last year of exile was one of the greatest gifts God ever gave me.

CHAPTER 10

Triumphant Return

In July of 1969, Father returned to the Provincial House in Los Angeles to continue his work with the Claretian Guilds. The year before (in 1968) the old Provincial House (an English Tudor style) was torn down because of old age and lack of good planning. During that same year, a brand new Provincial House (a Spanish style) was built on the same location (1119 Westchester Place). This new building has much more space and better planning for meetings and retreats than the old building had.

At that time, when Father returned to Los Angeles, I still did not know my vocation in life. So, I joined the U.S. Navy. For the next eight years, I served as an intelligence clerk in the navy. When I left Father, in 1969, Charles Carpenter replaced me as Father's next personal secretary.

The return of Father Aloysius to Los Angeles was crowned in a very special way. The newly chosen auxiliary bishop of Los Angeles, Bishop Arzube, chose Father as his chaplain at his consecration ceremony. That ceremony was on television throughout the whole Los Angeles area. It took place on March 25, of 1971 (Feastday of Mary's Annunciation). I happened to be home at my parents' house in Pomona that day, and was able to see Father Aloysius on TV at the side of Bishop Arzube.

The next day, I told Father I had seen him on TV at the ceremony in the Cathedral. Father smiled at me and said that the same men, who had expelled him, were there too. They were forced to see Father back in Los Angeles and in a place of honor. They saw him now with a powerful friend and protector, Bishop Arzube. Father's return to Los Angeles was now final, and truly triumphant!

Father was very active again. Crowds of people flocked to the new Provincial House for his Masses and his blessings. They would completely fill the large meeting room called the basement, with several hundred people each time. There were many cures and conversions through Father's blessings.

The New Provincial House was built in 1968. In it, Father Aloysius lived from 1969 to 1971, and 1973 to 1981.

CHAPTER 11

Surprise for an Atheist

With so many people coming to see him, Father at times liked to take a day off and go for what he called "an outing." On one such outing, a most remarkable thing happened.

In about 1970, Father went with two Carmelite nursing nuns, Mother Marguerite and Sister Mary Michael, on an outing to visit an orphanage. They went there to see Father Henry of the Passionists order, who was at an orphanage in the border town of Tecate, Mexico.

In front of the orphanage, they saw a young American man sitting there with his dog. The dog was missing one if its legs. Father Aloysius spoke to this stranger and told him: "You don't believe in God, but I will show you there is a God." The stranger said: "How?" Father told him: "Bring me your dog here." The stranger carried his dog to Father in his arms because it was missing one of its legs. Father began blessing the dog in the same place where the leg was missing. Suddenly, the missing leg materialized into a normal leg. This miracle was seen by all four of them: Father, Mother Marguerite, Sister Mary Michael, the stranger, and of course, the dog too. Father and the two nuns then walked into the orphanage, leaving the stranger totally amazed at what had just happened.

Father Aloysius did not like the disbelief of miracles that is so commonplace today. He said that there is too much belief that everything is purely natural. Father himself did not believe in the theory of natural evolution. He told me: "What evolution? It never happened!" Of course, this is a controversial subject. The Church permits some beliefs about it, and other beliefs are not permitted (like the evolution of the soul, that matter always existed, etc.). Pope Pius XII said this theory should be treated honestly, with the negative arguments against it given equal time. However, this is not the case in schools today.

Father told me to read books against the theory and I did. These books are called "Creation Science." They argue against natural evolution, in favor of a quick creation by God. They ask excellent questions like: "How could the chaos of a 'Big Bang' explosion just naturally turn into the wonderful order of stars, planets, and moons, all following such perfect orbits? How could the first living cell simply bring itself together, give itself a membrane skin, and then give itself the power to reproduce? Why is this not seen today? Where are all the missing links that do not exist today, nor in the fossil record?"

The fossil levels, according to Creation Science, are not the order of natural evolution, but rather are the order of burial in the world-wide Flood of Noah. The world is still 80% covered by water from that flood. Today's land and mountains were uplifted out of the flood. If they were lowered, the world would easily be covered by water again.

Evolutionists say that similarities between animals prove that they had common ancestors. But, the similarities only prove a common Designer - God. Evolution, according to Father and to me, is just another mistaken theory in the long history of scientific mistakes.

Father Aloysius admitted that he could be mistaken at times in his own personal opinions. Therefore, sometimes it was difficult to know if he was just expressing his own opinion, or if he actually had some divine insight into the same matter. Although Father admitted to being mistaken at times, it seems to me that this happened very rarely.

CHAPTER 12

At Fatima

A mong the strong opinions Father had, one was that priests, brothers, and nuns should wear religious clothing, called habits. Father said that the religious habit is "God's uniform." Father was very unhappy to see his fellow Claretians beginning to wear their habit (the cassock) less and less.

Another opinion of Father's was that religious should spend a lot of time in prayer. With this in mind, Father made plans to start a house of prayer at the Shrine of Fatima in Portugal. He received permission to do this from the Claretian Father General in Rome. So, in October of 1971, Father, and ten young men as his novices, flew from Los Angeles to Portugal to begin their house of prayer at Fatima. At first, they lived at the Portuguese Claretian Novitiate, which was a large building behind the Basilica. Father's group wore their habits (black cassocks) almost all the time, but the Portuguese Claretian novices in the same building did not. So, a few months later, the Claretian Father General in Rome sent Father Aloysius a letter that he received on February 9, 1972. In it, he told Father Aloysius that he should start his own order with his group of novices. Father was very happy about this. He and his group moved out of the Claretian Novitiate into a smaller, independent building, where they started their own, new community.

When they first arrived in Fatima, the bishop there was very favorable to them. But suddenly, that bishop resigned. Now there was a new bishop, who was not favorable towards them. He told Father Aloysius he would not give approval to his new order. His reason was that there was only one elderly priest (Father Aloysius) in poor health. If Father suddenly died, his group of young men would be without a leader and without a priest.

Father Aloysius was devastated by this news. Without the approval of the bishop, there could be no new order. His group, called Missionaries of Perpetual Adoration, had to be disbanded. Some of these young men joined other seminaries. Others simply returned home, giving up their dreams of the religious life.

One of the group, Charles Carpenter, decided to carry on Father's new order. He chose to attend the seminary in Burgos, Spain, in whose chapel Father Aloysius had been ordained a priest in 1929. Charles attended this seminary from 1973 to 1978.

Meanwhile, the Bishop of Ciudad Obregon in Mexico, heard about Father's order and the need of a bishop's approval. He talked with Father Aloysius in Los Angeles in 1977. This bishop then gladly gave his approval. The next year in 1978, this same bishop ordained Charles Carpenter a priest in Mexico. The Bishop assigned him and the new order to the town of Alamos. This order now has five priests today, with a number of others who will be ordained in the next few years. In remembrance of their origin at Fatima, this order is also called Missionaries of Fatima. Their address is:

Misioneros de Fatima
Apartado 44
Alamos, Sonora
85763 Mexico

In August of 1973, Father returned from Fatima to the Claretian Provincial House in Los Angeles. Officially, he had never left the Claretian order. He was only on extended leave to Fatima, for the two years that he was there. Returning to Los Angeles, Father felt that he had failed at Fatima. However, in a few years, he was to see the success take place in Mexico. It seems to me that Father's new order was more needed in Mexico than in Fatima. It also seems that Father himself was more needed in Los Angeles than in Fatima too.

CHAPTER 13

His Last Years

When Father Aloysius returned to Los Angeles from Fatima in 1973, he was reassigned back to his Claretian Guilds. His many friends were happy he was back with them again.

Father had already taken pilgrimage groups to Europe in 1968 and 1970. Now he was able to do so again, in 1975 and 1976. In 1976, he was also able to take his group to the Holy Land. This was to be his last pilgrimage and it gave him great joy to finally visit the Holy Land. However, while there, he suffered mystically, as he walked along the Way of the Cross in Jerusalem.

The next year, in 1977, Father made a special visit to my parents' house in Pomona. My father had become Father Aloysius' dentist from 1969 to 1979. Thus, my parents had invited Father to their home for dinner. I had gotten out of the Navy after eight years of service (1969 to 1977), and returned to California to live. At dinner that night, I was there with my wife, Jacinta, whom I had married in Spain the year before. Father looked at her and told her in Spanish: "Jeff didn't know his vocation in life. But when he married you, his eyes were opened." Interiorly, that is exactly what I felt.

Later, Father told me in private how much he liked the soul of my wife. He said her soul is "very special."

My wife and I went to visit Father at times at the Claretian Provincial House. We also attended his Masses at San Conrado Mission, located near Dodger Stadium. This small church was built by Father Thomas Matin C.M.F. (1900-1975). The saintly Father Matin had been the confessor and the friend of Father Aloysius for many years.

On January 7, 1979, my father died suddenly of a heart attack. Father Aloysius came for his rosary and his funeral at St. Joseph's

Church in Pomona. Father also blest his grave at Holy Cross Cemetery. At the cemetery, Father told me: "We all have to die. My time will come two to three years from now." (Father died two years and three months later). It had made me sad to hear Father say this to me. He also said that he had already had several small heart attacks. He said that the doctors had told him that he could die from heart failure at any moment.

During his last years, Father did receive consolations at times. However, Father thought it was more important that we should be a consolation to the suffering Christ by trying to live good lives. Father's favorite painting was "The Angel of Consolation." I was with him in 1968, when he bought that painting. Father pointed to the angel in the painting, who was consoling Christ during His agony in the garden. Father said: "We should be like that angel and console Christ by living lives that are pleasing to him. His all-knowing mind (during the agony in the garden) saw our lives today." Father believed that our good lives today would be acts of consolation to Christ, suffering in the garden, two thousand years ago.

Another great consolation to Father was the celebration of his Golden Jubilee of 50 years as a priest. This took place on November 3, 1979, at Good Shepherd Church in Beverly Hills. It was in this same church, the year before (in 1978), that the funeral of Queen Nazli had taken place.

For his Golden Jubilee, Father concelebrated Mass with Bishop Arzube and Bishop Moreno. My wife and I attended, along with several hundred other people. Afterwards, we all went to the Beverly Hilton Hotel nearby to have a luncheon in honor of Father. He was very moved by this outpouring of so many of his friends.

After this, Father's health was bad at times. He had become diabetic, besides his heart problems. At times, he was in the hospital, or at a convalescent home. When he was feeling better, he would return to the Provincial House, where his priestly blessing would continue to cure others.

Father could have retired from public life, but he chose not to do so. He wanted to serve God, by helping others, until the very end. And the end finally came for him on April 6, 1981. Father died at St. John's Hospital in Santa Monica, the same place where he had been cured twenty years earlier.

Father suffers mystically along the Way of the Cross in Jerusalem in June, 1976, as members of his pilgrimage group look on.

Father Aloysius: Wonder Worker in America

CHAPTER 14

His Death and After

B ecause Father died on an April 6, this date would be his feastday if he is ever canonized a saint. For a saint, the day of his death is the day of his birth into Heaven. Therefore, the Church celebrates the day of death as the feastday of a saint.

My wife and I went to see Father's body during visitation hours at the mortuary. I held our five-month old baby daughter, Maria, in my arms, as she looked down on Father's face. She also had been an answer to one of Father's prayers.

Father's funeral Mass was three days after his death. It was on a Thursday night, at San Gabriel Church, located to the right of the old mission. Since I was needed at work that night, I could not attend. Some who did attend, including Mrs. Morrow, told me that Bishop Arzube said something very special. He said: "We've already been contacted by Father Aloysius, and he says: 'No one can imagine how Heaven is! It's worth every sacrifice to get there!'"

Bishop Arzube did not explain to whom, nor how, Father Aloysius had made this contact from Heaven. But I do know that since his death, Father has appeared to several people in their dreams, while they were sleeping. Usually, what Father had to say was: "Ask me for my prayers. You will have need of them."

Father's funeral Mass had San Gabriel Church packed full of people. Mrs. Morrow estimated that there were over a thousand people inside the church, and also several hundred more people outside in front of the church. The next morning, for Father's rosary and burial, the church was almost full. My wife, baby daughter, and I were able to attend, and so, we were all there. After the rosary in the church, we accompanied Father's coffin for his burial in the mission garden. There Father is buried today with his fellow Claretians. His tomb is often visited by many people.

Five months after his burial, in September of 1981, Father was seen in either an apparition, or as a materialization, doing a good work. He had promised he would return to do good works from Heaven, and he did just that. He was seen walking out the front entrance of Mercy Hospital in San Diego, after having visited a dying friend. The friend was his fellow Basque, Mr. Al Esparza, who was dying there. Mr. Esparza's daughter (Mrs. Lisa Tobias) and her husband saw Father come walking out of the hospital, and he passed right next to them. Lisa turned to her husband and said: "That's Father Aloysius!" When they looked back to see him, he had already disappeared into thin air. They did not know yet that Father had died five months earlier.

Death has not stopped the healing power of God through the intercession of Father Aloysius. In 1991, Mrs. Sally Labadie received a cure through Father's intercession. That year she had a serious problem with her stomach muscles. She could hardly walk. She went to Father's tomb and asked him for his prayers to cure her. The next morning, she woke up completely cured. In 1995, I went with a friend (Mr. Robert Queen) and his wife to Father's tomb to pray with them to seek Father's intercession for a healing they sought. While praying at Father's tomb my friend experienced Father's gift of mystical aroma. Later that evening he became aware that he had received an interior healing of a problem that had affected him for over thirty years. God is still using Father Aloysius to heal His hurting children on earth today.

People should ask Father Aloysius for his intercession and help in Heaven. If they receive a miracle, they should send their testimony to:

> Provincial Superior
> Claretians
> 1119 Westchester Pl.
> Los Angeles, CA 90019

The Claretians have not yet taken steps to open an investigation of Father as a possible candidate for sainthood, although they should. They have jurisdiction over it. I believe they should do something on behalf of Father, for he certainly did an immense amount of good on their behalf.

Father's tomb is located in the mission garden at
San Gabriel Mission, in San Gabriel, California.

Father Aloysius: Wonder Worker in America

CHAPTER 15

In the Apocalypse

It was revealed to the great miracle-worker, St. Vincent Ferrer (1350-1418), that he was the Sixth Angel of the Apocalypse. Likewise, it was revealed to St. Anthony Claret (1807-1870) that he was the Seventh Angel, described in Chapter 10. He wrote about this only because of his obedience to his spiritual director. St. Anthony Claret wrote that the "Seven Thunders who uttered their voices are those other preachers who will follow me."

It seems that "those preachers" would be holy priests like St. Anthony Claret himself. He had mystical gifts and worked miracles. It seems that the "Seven Thunders" would do the same. Like thunder, they would also echo throughout the world in different nations. Perhaps, for France the thunder was Pere Lamy (1853-1931), for Italy Padre Pio (1887-1968) and for the United States Father Aloysius (1905-1981).

Continuing along with the theme of the Apocalypse, Father Aloysius said it was better that he die then, rather to live on to see the things that are to come. The disasters that are to come are found in Chapter 16 of the Apocalypse. They were also claimed to have been seen in visions given during the 1960's at the village of Garabandal in Spain.

It was Father Aloysius who taught me what the word "Garabandal" means. He told me it comes from his native Basque language and means the "high place." The Basque word for "high" is "Garai." The spelling and pronunciation of "Garabandal" is Basque, slightly changed down through the centuries. This village is located in a Castillian province, just west of the Basque country in Spain.

The villiage of Garabandal is located in a "high place" in a beautiful, isolated mountain valley. It's located an hour drive south-west of the city of Torrelavega. Father Aloysius visited Garabandal in 1970, and he was very pleased about it.

In 1972, two of the four visionary girls of Garabandal went to see Father Aloysius, while he was living at Fatima in Portugal. Father read their souls and saw the truth of their visions. Father Aloysius confirmed this to Father Charles Carpenter, Mike Murphy, yourself, and others. At Garabandal, the Blessed Virgin Mary showed the future as follows:

1. First there will come a sudden crisis in the world, with civil turmoil. During it, there will be a persecution of the Church and priests will be forced into hiding. This crisis will be widespread in the world, and not just in one country alone.

2. Then God will send a world-wide warning. It will be seen in the sky and in the air around us. There will be a lot of light and noise, waking up the other half of the world that is still sleeping. The shock of it will force everyone on earth to think about the state of their soul and their conscience. With everyone's attention going inward, everything outward will appear to have stopped. It will seem that all movement has stopped, with only silence and a feeling of emptiness all around. Then suddenly, everything will continue normally as it was before. This whole experience, called the Warning, will not directly cause injury nor death. It will be a terror of short duration. Christ has already prophesied that there will come "Terrors from Heaven." (Luke 21:1), and this could well be one of them.

3. After the Warning, there will be a miracle at Garabandal, proving that the apparitions that happened there were true. The local bishops (of Santander) have neither approved, nor condemned them so far. Church law permits personal belief in unapproved apparitions, provided they contain nothing contrary to Church doctrine.

4. Sometime after the Miracle happens at Garabandal, there will come a world-wide chastisement upon the sinful and unrepentant of this world. The visions seemed to be from Chapter 16 of the Apocalypse: "the wrath of God upon the earth ... rivers made

blood ... men afflicted with heat and fire ... water dried up." These events all seemed tied together into one great chastisement. Christ said that there will come a "great tribulation as never before ... unless those days be shortened, no flesh should be saved: but for the sake of the elect those days shall be shortened." (Matt. 24:22) Other things that may be a part of it could be the "distress of nations" by the roaring of the sea and waves, (Luke 21:25) and such a great earthquake that the cities of the Gentiles fell, Apoc. 16 and the sun shall be darkened. (Matt. 24:29)

Blessed Anna Mari Taigi (1769-1837) prophesied details of a world-wide chastisement, which she called the "Three Days of Darkness." At Garabandal, when the visions of the chastisement began, everything in the vision turned dark. There was also seen fire in the sky. In the Bible, it is prophesied that: "two parts of the earth shall perish, but the third part shall be left. I (God) will bring the third part through the fire." (Zacharius 13:8) These things will happen. The Bible says so. Plus from Garabandal is the prophecy: "Without expecting it, the Chastisement *will come.*"

5. After the Chastisement, the next event is the conversion of the survivors. From Garabandal is the prophecy: "The whole human race will enter the Catholic Church." The Blessed Virgin Mary also said we should pray for this intention, indicating the Catholic Faith is the one true faith. A little-known Spanish mystic of the last century put this in a beautiful way: "The Catholic Faith will become the *happiness* of the whole human race." Christ Himself said: "There will be one fold (one Church)," (John 10:16)

With the gospel finally made known throughout the "whole world, the end will come." (Matt. 24:14) The Church says the last years at the end of the world will be ruled by the evil Anti-Christ, followed by Christ's Second Coming, the Resurrection of the Dead, and the Last Judgment.

Meanwhile, we should take advantage of the time God gives us to serve Him well in this life, so as to be happy with Him in the next. This is what the life of Father Aloysius was all about. With Father we have an example that will last forever.

Father's Life

June 21, 1905   Born at Yurre in Vizcaya Province, Spain.

1905 - 1916   Childhood at Yurre.

1916 - 1930   Studied at Claretian seminaries in Spain.

Nov. 29, 1929   Ordained a priest at Burgos by the archbishop.

1930 - 1931   Priest assisting at Cathedral of Panama City, Panama.

April 25, 1931   Entered the U.S.A. by ship at San Diego, California.

1931 - 1942   Teacher at Claretian seminaries in U.S.A.

Mar. 21, 1940   (Holy Thursday) Received gifts of reading hearts and of curing in Chapel of Our Lady's Academy, Manteno, Illinois.

April 10, 1941   (Holy Thursday) Received gift of Sacramental Species (becoming a living tabernacle) at Novitiate Chapel of the Sisters of the Holy Heart of Mary, at Beaverville, Il.

1942 - 1943   Master of Novices in Walnut, California.

1943 - 1948   Teacher at Dominguez Seminary, Compton, CA

1948 - 1957   Master of Novices in Los Angeles, CA.

1957 - 1963   Founder & Moderator of 12 Claretian Guilds in Los Angeles, California.

1963 - 1969   Pastor of parishes in Arizona and Texas.

1969 - 1971   Moderator of 12 Claretian Guilds in Los Angeles.

1971 - 1973   Founder & Superior of Missionaries of Perpetual Adoration, at Fatima, Portugal.

1973 - 1981   Moderator of Claretian Guilds in Los Angeles, California.

April 6, 1981   Died at St. John's Hospital, at Santa Monica, California.

April 9, 1981   Funeral Mass at San Gabriel Church, San Gabriel, California.

April 10, 1981   Burial in the Claretian Cemetery in the garden of San Gabriel Mission, at San Gabriel, California.